Original title:
A Green World Indoors

Copyright © 2025 Creative Arts Management OÜ
All rights reserved.

Author: Evan Hawthorne
ISBN HARDBACK: 978-1-80581-748-2
ISBN PAPERBACK: 978-1-80581-275-3
ISBN EBOOK: 978-1-80581-748-2

Nature's Embrace

In pots and beds, the herbs do sing,
Basil's sass starts a wild fling.
Cacti tease with prickly smiles,
While ivy climbs and runs for miles.

A fern declares, 'I'm king today!'
As socks go missing in the fray.
Plants gossip softly, which is worse,
A broken stem or friend in verse?

Verdant Whispers

A tiny sprout with big dreams sees,
It's growing up to be like peas.
Lettuce laughs, 'I love this light!'
While mushrooms hide from morning bright.

The rubber plant wears boots of green,
And whispers secrets, smooth and clean.
With every breeze, they dance and twirl,
Oh what a sight, this leafy whirl!

The Lush Sanctuary

The pothos drapes like a diva bold,
Dancing around like it owns the fold.
Spider plants stretch with flair and style,
As if to say, 'Stay here a while!'

A peace lily blushes, looking shy,
While succulents flaunt 'We don't need to cry!'
Together they play, a vibrant crew,
Making indoor dreams seem fresh and new!

In Bloom Beneath Glass

Behind the panes, the flowers grin,
They've heard the gossip of wild wind.
Petunias flirt, while daisies wink,
In this glass house, plants never think!

Chrysanthemums pull their best poses,
As ferns giggle with shiny roses.
In this fun jungle minus the mud,
Joy blossoms like a playful bud!

Sheltered in Green

In corners, plants dance and sway,
Ferns wear hats made of clay.
Cacti grin with prickly cheer,
While trees laugh, growing near.

Pothos climbs the curtain rod,
Sipping sunlight like a god.
Spider plants twirl and prance,
Creating quite the leafy dance.

Lettuce dreams of leafy fame,
While basil plays a herb-filled game.
The orchids gossip, feeling proud,
In this indoor plant-filled crowd.

Fiddle leaf figs pull funny faces,
As rubber plants find their places.
Together they share their skills,
In this home of joyous thrills.

The Indoor Eden

In pots and vases, life does bloom,
Bringing joy to every room.
Succulents with a wink and nod,
Look more like statues, quite odd.

A snake plant tries to sneak a peek,
At all the flowers, feeling chic.
There's laughter in this leafy scene,
As violets can't help but preen.

A hanging ivy swings with glee,
Tickling toes of guests, you see.
Herbs are plotting kitchen tricks,
While daisies share their funny quips.

Sunlight pours and plants convene,
In this indoor jungle green.
With every leaf, a quirky tale,
Of joy that never seems to pale.

Petals in the Parlor

Petals in the parlor sprawl,
As potted pals have a ball.
The roses waltz with ferns in tow,
While violets giggle, putting on a show.

A peace lily offers up a joke,
Making fun of a sleepy oak.
"Why don't you move?" she pokes with grace,
"I'd win a race in this plant race!"

Bamboo shoots stretch and try to play,
Limbo contest on display!
The orchids cheer and root for fun,
In this parlor, everyone's won.

A curious bug joins in the frolic,
Adding laughter, quite symbolic.
Here in this vibrant, leafy land,
Laughter flourishes, oh so grand!

Leafy Reverie

In whispers soft, the leaves do speak,
In a world that's far from bleak.
Dieffenbachia shares a plot,
While happy herbs cook up a thought.

Anthurium wears a flashy hat,
While rubber plants say, "How about that?"
With every leaf, a silly wink,
In this green space, we all think.

The blinds are drawn, it's all quite bright,
As plants tell tales into the night.
With laughter echoing in the air,
Every creature joins the fair.

In this leafy dream, they twine,
Creating joys that intertwine.
Here, every leaf is fun to see,
In this whimsical greenery!

Indoor Eden Emerging

In a pot sits a cactus, quite prickly and nice,
Who claims he feels lonely, oh, isn't that twice?
While ferns wave their fronds like they're having a ball,
"He's not that cute," says the spider plant tall.

A sunflower dreams of the sun's warm embrace,
While succulents giggle at their slow-growing race.
A rubber tree sighs, 'I'm so flexible too!'
But the peace lily shrieks, 'We're all just bamboo!'

Shadows of the Houseplant

In the corner, a pothos is plotting a scheme,
To strangle the drapes with its green, leafy dream.
The snake plant whispers, 'I'm tough and I'm sly,'
Yet terracotta pots always catch them awry.

The monsteras dance with their glossy, green hues,
Creating a ruckus in their leafy, chic shoes.
Oh, the joys of the shadows and plant-based delight,
Where every green stalk gets into mischief at night.

The Verdure Above My Head

An air plant dangles, with such pompous pride,
It claims it's the crown that I simply can't hide.
With its wild, curly tendrils swaying in cheer,
It giggles, 'Join me, there's nothing to fear!'

My ceiling's a jungle, or maybe a maze,
Where vines seek the light, in a glorious craze.
Each leaf tells a story, so witty and spry,
Who knew such green antics were happening up high?

Blossoms in the Air

With blossoms in the air, there's a chaos of blooms,
As orchids gossip about the plant shop's rooms.
A hyacinth grins, 'I smell way too sweet,'
While the wilted petunia just can't find her feet.

The violets brag of their bright, purple flair,
While daisies tease them for their lack of fresh hair.
Together they laugh in their floral domain,
In this funny indoor garden, it's never mundane!

The Cozy Canopy

In the corner, a plant does dance,
Misplaced at first, it took a chance.
Leaves like fans, swaying in glee,
Who knew they'd thrive with such jubilee?

Spider plants plotting a takeover spree,
Whispering secrets, just wait and see.
I water them, they give me sass,
I'm the gardener, they've got some class!

Growth Amidst the Concrete

In a pot, a cactus rolls its eyes,
"I'm tough!" it boasts, in its prickly guise.
Neighbors laugh, "It's all a show!"
But we know, it's not just for show!

Ferns in the hall, are having a ball,
They gossip together, all leafy and tall.
"Did you see that pot? Not quite my style,
But I'll make it work; it's just for a while!"

Tender Tending in Silence

A rubber plant's style is quite the delight,
It wears its sheen, oh, what a sight!
Sometimes it seems to roll its eyes,
Wondering why I'm so full of sighs.

The peace lily nods, quite sage and wise,
"Just talk to us more, and we'll arise."
But I trip over pots, with footwear quite bright,
They giggle and chuckle oh what a sight!

A Breath of Fresh Air

A window ajar, with a breeze that's sly,
Sneaks in through curtains, gives plants a high.
"Do you feel that?" the basil does grin,
"I'm growing so tall, it's a win-win!"

Succulents smirk, thinking they're cool,
"Water us too much? What a fool!
We bask in the sun, a true sunbather,
Keeping it green, while we snack on vapor!

Blooms in the Heart of the House

In corners where the sunlight plays,
A cactus wears a sunhat, always sways.
The fern forgot how to be neat,
Turns every day into a frilly treat.

The cat thinks plants are gobbling treats,
While chewing on those leafy feats.
A shower of leaves, a greenery spree,
Plants giggle, 'We're just here for the tea!'

Tulips prance like they own the room,
Whispering secrets as they loom.
A pot of herbs sparks joy and cheer,
Basil whispers, 'I'm the coolest here!'

In every nook, our friends reside,
With blooming laughter, they abide.
Who needs a gardener's skillful hands?
These playful pots have their own plans!

Nature's Touch of Interiors

A vine climbs high just to explore,
While rubber plants look for the door.
With peeking leaves and playful roots,
They send us jokes in funny suits.

The sunflower wears a goofy grin,
As if he is the captain of this din.
Hiding gnomes from flowerpot seas,
Yelling, 'We're here to bring you peace!'

On rainy days, balloons of moss,
Bounce around, they're never at a loss.
The orchids sigh, 'We're too divine,'
While ferns say, 'Who needs a wine?'

A tiny bug plays hide and seek,
In a peace lily's soft, gentle creek.
Nature's jokes fill every space,
In this wild indoor heart's embrace!

Soft Cradles of Photosynthesis

Green pillows line the living room,
Next to them, plants cut the gloom.
A jade plant cracks a smile today,
Saying, 'Come, let's dance and sway!'

The leaves are busy, making food,
Joking, 'Life's a chlorophyll mood!'
Dust bunnies watch with envy, sigh,
'Why can't we wear the green… oh my!'

Silly succulents stacked up high,
Wobble when a pet walks by.
Each leaf a twist, a little tease,
In this soft cradle of photosynthesis ease.

Kitchen herbs play chef with flair,
Cilantro spins in a lively air.
Why can't we throw a plant parade?
With dandelions, let's serenade!

The Comfort of Growing Things

Plants around me dance with glee,
They wiggle and they sway; you see,
Each leaf a hand, waving hello,
In my jungle, I'm the star of the show.

I water them while sipping tea,
They shout, "More water!" just like me.
Sometimes I swear they tell me jokes,
Or maybe it's just the sneaky smoke.

My cat plots schemes to chase a leaf,
While I'm stuck here, in disbelief.
Do they conspire, those green-eyed foes?
Or just nudge me when boredom grows?

As pots accumulate dust and grime,
I laugh, capturing nature in rhyme.
These friends don't mind my silly quirks,
With every stem, a world of perks.

Reflecting on Green Spaces

In a corner, plants are reflecting,
Their shiny leaves are all connecting.
I swear they gossip, share their tales,
While I munch on popcorn, as a snack prevails.

My spider plant throws a party,
Inviting succulents, oh so hearty.
They shimmy on the windowsill,
And hold their breaths, all quiet and still.

Cacti bicker on who's prickliest,
While herbs debate, who's the zestiest.
I chuckle at my indoor zoo,
Where the wildest critters have a view.

With my watering can like a scepter,
I rule this kingdom, the ultimate vector.
These lush companions, a delight to see,
Planting smiles, growing glee.

An Enclave of Indoor Life

Here in my kingdom of leafy greens,
I crown my fern, split ends and scenes.
It whispers softly, to my delight,
"Just water me more, and I'll be bright!"

In the shadows, my pothos creeps,
Plotting secrets while the sunlight sleeps.
I drop crumbs for my tiny pals,
In hopes they give me new green styles.

The orchids, too, are quite the crowd,
They flaunt their colors, humble but proud.
As I dance around, in socks, no shoes,
They cheer me on, sharing my views.

Each day brings new sproutling tales,
While the kitchen hums with gentle gales.
Together we thrive, non-stop and bold,
A band of plants, in stories told.

Colors of Indoor Eden

Here's a jungle, built with flair,
Where colors burst from every chair!
My hibiscus blushes, like it's shy,
While my snake plant shoots for the sky.

Potpourri of shades, wild and bright,
A canvas that brings sheer delight.
As the sunlight dances on my skin,
I imagine a world where plants can grin.

Ferns wear polka dots, isn't that neat?
While violets vie for a cozy seat.
Together we bloom in this indoor place,
Where every inch is a vibrant grace.

But watch the cat, he's on a spree,
Chasing shadows, plotting glee.
This colorful life, a comical spree,
In a world where nature dances free.

Ferns Whispering in Quiet Rooms

In the corner, ferns do sway,
Whispering secrets in a playful way.
They gossip about the dust bunnies,
And share jokes about the sun and honey.

With leaves that dance like silly clowns,
They mock the plants that wear sad frowns.
"Why grow taller? That's such a bore,"
Says the fern that sprawls upon the floor.

They giggle when the sunlight bends,
Making shadows that twist and blend.
"Oh look! A tree in a worm's disguise!"
They chuckle as they roll their eyes.

So if you hear a fern's bright laugh,
Just know they're sharing the best half.
Of all the joys of living earth,
In quiet rooms, they find their mirth.

Sheltered by Leaves

Under thick leaves, a shy plant hides,
Wearing a crown made of leafy tides.
"I'm the ruler of this little turf!"
It claims while pretending to be tough.

Its neighbors giggle, "What a whim!
We know you're really quite a dim!"
The pots shake with laughter all around,
As the mischievous vines take their ground.

"Let's throw a party!" the ferns reply,
"We'll dance and sway and touch the sky!"
The shy one blushes, "I'm not so bold…"
Yet soon it joins, as happiness unfolds.

Now the leaves rustle in vibrant cheer,
In the cozy spot where all feel near.
A leafy shelter, a joyful trance,
In the green surprise, they twist and dance!

The Homegrown Symphony

In the window, herbs are singing,
Basil is crowing, thyme is swinging.
"Let's start a band!" the mint does shout,
While rosemary's trying to figure it out.

The pots perform a wobbly tune,
With parsley bouncing to the moon.
The carrots are clapping, holding the beat,
As the radish tries to find its feet.

"Here comes the chorus!" the lettuce yells,
While the peas pop up and ring their bells.
The whole kitchen joins in their merry song,
As the aroma swirls and rights the wrong.

So if you hear a playful croon,
Know it's just greens rocking 'til noon.
In pots and planters, joy is grown,
A homegrown symphony all its own!

Verdant Echoes of the Heart

In every leaf, a story beats,
Of playful roots and silly treats.
"Did you hear how the cactus blushed?"
When it saw the fern all green and rushed!

Echoes of laughter bounce off the walls,
As potted pals share their leafy calls.
"Let's throw a shindig in the sun!"
Cheerful chaos is now begun.

The orchids prance in elegant style,
While the succulents grin from a mile.
"Join our dance!" the ivy pleads,
Twisting and twirling in joyful beads.

So here's to the green with giggles galore,
In every corner, there's always more.
Hear the echoes, feel the fun,
In the verdant heart, we're all one.

Sunlit Serenity

In the corner, a plant does sway,
Chasing dust bunnies all day.
Leaves waving hello with a grin,
While the cat plots her win.

Basil dreams of pizza night,
Thyme thinks it's out of sight.
Cacti throwing shade just so,
While the drapes steal the show.

Sunbeams dance on the floor,
As my fern begs for more.
A rubber plant holds court, aghast,
Watching laundry that's amassed.

Laughs echo from the room,
With my plants in full bloom.
In this jungle, we play, oh my,
Only need one more chai!

Cultivated Corners

In the kitchen, pots collide,
Mint and cilantro take a ride.
Fiddle leaf's a drama queen,
Acting like she's never seen.

Sage and rosemary jest,
Competing for the best dressed.
A tiny gnome keeps a watchful eye,
While the orchids practice their sigh.

My cactus throws a party loud,
Inviting all from the crowd.
Soil gets tossed, it's a grand mess,
Who knew gardening's a stress?

Hilarious green in every spot,
Each corner overflowing a lot.
With laughter and cheer, they cheerfully sprout,
Cozy gatherings are what it's about!

Soft Shadows of Ivy

Ivy climbs with stealthy grace,
Scaling walls, finding its place.
Whispers softly to the vine,
"Let's create a leafy line!"

Spider plants play hide and seek,
While the pothos starts to sneak.
Twisting round the window's ledge,
Like a garden-themed hedge.

Snake plants lend their stoic flair,
Acting tough, they truly care.
My fern does yoga, bendy and spry,
While succulents giggle, letting out a sigh.

Through the shadows where they dwell,
Frolicking in their leafy shell.
Together they plot, oh such a fuss,
Creating a green world, just for us!

The Agora of Green

Gather round, the greens convene,
In a meeting, rarely seen.
Each with stories full of zest,
Of all the dirt and what's the best!

Petunias gossip, wrinkled leaves,
While geraniums roll up their sleeves.
Citrus bursts with zesty cheer,
As tomatoes shed a tear.

Ferns trade tips on shade and light,
While the daisies keep it bright.
Cacti nod with prickly pride,
As the herbs dance side by side.

Join the cacti's quirky parade,
In this indoor leafy escapade.
With laughter and charm, let it be known,
This green agora can't be outshone!

Verdant Dreams Beneath Glass

Tiny leaves dance with glee,
Caught in a sunlit spree.
They sip on water, so divine,
Whispering hopes for a steep incline.

In pots they throw their leafy hats,
Competing with my lazy cats.
'We're the stars,' they chirp and beam,
While I just plot my lunchtime dream.

Fingers green, they shimmy and twist,
Beneath the glass, they can't resist.
A mini jungle in my den,
Where lizards come to take a pen!

I chuckle as they stretch and yawn,
While dust bunnies plot to fawn.
Our leafy pals toss out their flair,
In this charming indoor affair.

Ferns in the Sunlight

Ferns peek out, with fronds so sly,
Doing yoga, oh my oh my!
They pose in sunlight, green and bright,
Like plants on a runway, what a sight!

Got a fern who thinks it's a dog,
Chasing shadows, like a log.
When I say 'stay,' it gives a frown,
Just leans a bit, won't fall down!

A battle with dust, they wage each day,
Hoping for nourishment, come what may.
I toss in some notes, make a wish,
They nod, they twist – oh, what a dish!

Ferns in the sunlight sing with cheer,
Inviting all to come and peer.
With fun and laughter brewed in pots,
It seems that silliness really connects the dots.

Secrets of the Potted Sanctuary

In the corner, a sanctuary peaked,
Whispers of leaves, oh how they creaked!
They plot their world with cheeky grouse,
Looking quite pleased in their small house.

The spider plant plays peek-a-boo,
While silly succulents stick like glue.
'No humans allowed!' they seem to say,
As I sip tea, they laugh and sway.

In shadows they trade their pickled glee,
With all the gossip about old me.
'He really thinks he's the boss here!'
The blooms seem to chuckle, quietly near.

Their little quirks inspire and tease,
Making my day with playful ease.
In this green club no one's left out,
Just secrets shared, laughter, and doubt.

Roots in the Living Room

Roots in the living room, oh what a sight,
Snaking around, planning their flight.
They tickle my toes as I walk near,
Swaying and laughing, yes, quite the cheer!

My houseplants throw a weekly rave,
In pots and vases, they seem so brave.
With roots that wiggle and twist with flair,
Dancing around without a care.

They've taken control of the remote,
Making poor TV choices, I gloat.
'Why watch the news when we can prance?'
They join in for the second chance dance!

So here we sit, in our silly spree,
Plants in pajamas, wiggling with glee.
Roots in the living room, what a delight,
A family of greens, all ready for flight.

The Verdure Within

In my room, a plant does groove,
It dances as I bust a move.
With leaves that shimmy, bright and bold,
It's got more style than I, truth be told.

A cactus laughs, it tells a joke,
While leafy friends just sit and poke.
The fern's a fan of high-five cheer,
Though it just wiggles, I still adhere.

I water them, they soothe my soul,
Yet they plot to take control,
I swear that plant's a mastermind,
Next thing you know, we'll be entwined!

With sunlight streaming, laughter roams,
This quirky jungle feels like home.
In every leaf, a giggle grows,
My houseplants rule, and everybody knows!

Roots of Tranquility

A potter's clay, a sneaky sprout,
Roots tickle 'neath the floor, no doubt.
They spread like rumors, far and wide,
In search of snacks, no need to hide.

A peace lily whispers sweet refrain,
While succulents play the waiting game.
Cheers to the pals who never fuss,
Where's the plant? Oh, just don't rush!

The ivy climbs, it has ambition,
Chasing the light like it's on a mission.
And here I sit with no regrets,
Just a lounge chair—and plant pets!

A garden indoors, what a sight,
With laughter leafing, oh so bright!
In this leafy realm, we share a grin,
Who knew tranquility could be this win?

Green Dreams at Dusk

At dusk, my ferns spin tales quite grand,
With moonlight shining, they take a stand.
The spider plant, all dressed in white,
Says, "Dance with me beneath the night!"

My rubber tree, a grumpy chap,
Grows taller yet, is still a sap.
With dreams of fame, he poses tall,
But really, he just likes to sprawl.

The pots conspire, mischief in bloom,
As shadows waggle, filling the room.
Each leaf a secret, each root a scheme,
In this twilight magic, we weave a dream!

So here we are, in leafy jest,
With twinkling lights, we're surely blessed.
As night falls soft, the fun is prime,
A garden's giggle, lost in rhyme!

Subtle Sprouts

A tiny sprout in a cozy bowl,
Looks up with hope, it's got a goal.
"I'll be a tree, just wait and see!"
But right now, I'm just stuck with tea.

A basil plant dreams of cuisine,
Wants to be pesto, oh so clean.
But here it sits, with snips and snags,
Plotting its future with leafy jags.

The jade plant nods, wise and aware,
"You kids calm down, it's time to care!"
With patience, he suggests with flair,
"In time, you'll grow, just don't despair!"

Through trials of water, sun, and fun,
These subtle sprouts brighten everyone.
In this little world, where laughter bounces,
We thrive together, our joy announces!

Emerald Sanctuary

In the corner, a cactus waves,
A prickly dude, but oh, he saves.
Cheering up with a sunny grin,
Water him too much? Where to begin!

Ferns fiddle while the sunlight dances,
Pothos plans its leafy prances.
I trip on greens, my socks adorned,
In this jungle, I feel reborn.

My cat's in awe, she studies each leaf,
As if the plants are up to some mischief.
With every sip, I hear them cheer,
Make a toast to my leafy sphere!

A gnome in the pot, his hat askew,
He nods in agreement, if only he knew.
In this sanctuary, I find delight,
Who knew indoor plants could take flight?

Home Among the Leaves

A spider plant swings, thinks it's a star,
Hanging out like it's a plant bazaar.
Basil dreams of pesto, chipotle's fate,
While mint tries to vibe with a veggie plate.

I swear that fern is plotting my doom,
As I tiptoe past, it whispers, 'Gloom!'
Succulents smirk, with their thick, green skin,
'You forgot to water? Let the games begin!'

In this indoor jungle, there's no defeat,
Every leaf whispers secrets, oh so sweet.
Yet they all conspire when I leave the room,
Plotting a coup, oh the plant-based gloom!

Yet amid this chaos, I sip my tea,
Laughing at ferns, they don't deceive me.
Home among leaves, where fun never dies,
Just watch your step—watch the plant spies!

Room for Growth

In my small flat, it's lush and bright,
Leaves are waving; what a sight!
Every window a leafy show,
But why does the basil always grow slow?

I talk to my violets, they nod along,
Singing to them feels completely wrong.
But who can resist a leafy chat?
They giggle back, 'Where's the salad at?'

Cacti poke me with their tiny quips,
'Water us less, or face the whips!'
Blooms in the bathroom, a floral fest,
Who knew a shower could be such a quest?

So here I stand, a proud plant dad,
Proud of my jungle, happy, and glad.
There's room for growth in this space so neat,
Will someone please find the carpet to meet?

Flora's Retreat

My living room's a jungle gym,
With foliage thick and chances slim.
Plants plotting a coup, I hear them chatter,
'Let's break free!' they say, 'What's the matter?'

Aliens? Nah, just a green brigade,
Fighting for sunlight, their leafy crusade.
The succulents grumbling, the ferns take flight,
My armchair's a pitstop for their leafy rite.

The bamboo sways, like a dancing crew,
While ivy winks as if it knew.
I tell them stories, they nod and giggle,
In this flora retreat, there's always a wiggle.

So I take a seat, with popcorn in hand,
Looking at leaves, isn't it grand?
In Flora's retreat, the fun never ends,
Just hope they don't start gathering friends!

Chlorophyll Conversations

In the corner, a plant does sway,
Saying, 'Water me, please! Don't delay!'
With leaves that chat, in shades of bright,
I wonder if they argue day and night.

The cactus shouts, 'I'm tough and prickly!'
While the fern just giggles, feeling frilly.
They gossip about the cat's past plays,
As I listen in, in a daze of praise.

The basil whispers, 'Cook me right!'
While the thyme rolls its eyes at the sight.
The plot thickens as the sunlight beams,
In this leafy world where all are dreams.

Each stem a tale, each pot a scene,
This indoor jungle feels so serene.
Among these friends, who needs the sky?
With leafy laughter, we all get by.

Nature's Embrace Within

A fussy fern just loves to fuss,
While succulents say, 'You're making a fuss!'
The snake plant snoozes in its pot,
Dreaming of jungles, oh what a shot!

The lizard lounges, nonchalant and chill,
Sipping sun like it's a fancy thrill.
While minor mishaps, like soil spills,
Have resulted in hilarious thrills.

Do flowers laugh? I swear they do,
At my dance moves, now that's the view!
With petals fluttering, cheering my jig,
Even the cactus is tapping a big!

Join the party, oh leafy friends,
In our indoor haven, fun never ends.
As laughter blossoms, oh what a place,
Nature's embrace puts joy on my face.

Petals on My Window Sill

Petals giggle on the bright sill,
Demanding sunlight, throwing a thrill.
The geraniums play peek-a-boo,
While violets blush in morning dew.

My cat sneezes, oh what a sight!
Bouncing flowers in pure delight.
'Quit tickling me!' the rose then begs,
As laughter dances on tiny legs.

Toys of soil and water can flow,
It's a circus! This much I know.
Leaves are tightrope walkers today,
Making their moves in the most cheeky way.

So here we are, the petal crew,
Chatting and giggling, just me and you.
In this pot of mischief, no frown shall kill,
As joy blooms bright on my window sill.

The Cultivated Calm

In the corner, a herb garden thrives,
While the parsley jives, no one derives.
Mint giggles with every fresh breeze,
Swaying away with such leafy ease.

My aloe is wise, a sage so grand,
Counseling all with a gentle hand.
'Take it easy,' it says with a wink,
'Life is just better, don't overthink!'

As orchids pose with their regal flair,
Comically twisting, oh what a dare!
They plan fashion shows down on the mat,
With blooms that would make others go flat.

This cultivated calm is anything but,
It's a riot of growth, not a dull rut.
Between the laughs and leafy guise,
I chill with my plants, oh what a prize!

Secret Garden Shelters

In pots and planters, mischief brews,
A fern that tickles your funny shoes.
Cacti waving with prickly cheer,
Whispering secrets that only you hear.

A spider plant's dance, a leafy jig,
It laughs out loud, though it's quite big.
Hide and seek with a curious vine,
In this green circus, all things align.

Pothos dangling like a grapevine meme,
While the peace lily plots its next dream.
Here laughter grows alongside the shade,
Among leafy friends, worries are swayed.

So here we gather, laughing with greens,
In our leafy hideaway, absurdity leans.
A jungle of joy where silliness reigns,
Our secret garden, full of playful gains.

A Breath of Chlorophyll

A cactus in slippers and shades so cool,
Sipping on sunlight, it breaks every rule.
The leaves all gossip like old friends do,
    Telling tall tales of the clumsy dew.

Succulents smile with their rubbery grins,
Festival of greens where laughter begins.
A basil leaf's humor scents the air,
Whispering jokes with a fragrant flair.

The rubber plant squeaks with a sudden jig,
    Grooving to rhythms, just look at it dig!
A tiny pot of mint with a wicked laugh,
    May just lead to a herb-infused gaffe.

In this crowded space, fun takes the lead,
Plant parties flourish; we're all guaranteed.
With every bloom, the laughter shall flow,
    In this verdant zone, we steal the show.

Living Canopy

Beware the ferns, they plot with glee,
Their leafy layers hold jokes for free.
An avocado pear thinks it's so sly,
Dropping its puns as it waves goodbye.

The string of hearts dangles like gold,
Telling stories from days of old.
So many leaves, each one a hoot,
Confetti of green in this leafy boot.

A palm named Polly steals the scene,
With palm fronds dancing, oh so obscene!
A rubber tree giggles, bending with flair,
Prompting laughter, filling the air.

In this living canopy, we twirl around,
Among quirky greens, a party is found.
The laughter erupts like a springtime breeze,
In this green retreat, we're always at ease.

Indoor Oasis

In our indoor haven, the fun never sleeps,
With leafy companions, our laughter leaps.
Succulents smirk with their baked-on style,
While the ivy winks, making us smile.

A pot full of herbs concocts a plan,
For sneaky recipes, that's the span.
With a little bit of thyme and a dash of cheer,
They concoct the funniest dishes so near.

The peaceful bamboo holds secrets galore,
While telling us jokes about a lion's roar.
A fern flips its fronds with such finesse,
Wishing to join in the leafy jest.

In this oasis lush, fun grows on trees,
Tickling our fancy like a light summer breeze.
Each plant a partner in this joyful spree,
In our indoor world, we're forever carefree.

A Canvas of Nature

Potted plants are in a race,
Chasing sunlight, it's a chase!
Fern is plotting, oh so sly,
To hide the cactus, watch it fly!

Succulents dance in vibrant hues,
While ferns plot their leafy duels.
The spider plant weaves its tale,
As rubber trees start to swell.

A sunbeam slides across the floor,
The orchids can't resist a score.
They nod and wink, a cheeky crew,
In this indoor sunny zoo!

Verdurous Whispers of Life

In the corner sits a jade,
Whispering secrets, unafraid.
A tiny spider spins its web,
While all the other plants just ebb.

A peace lily sings a tune,
While violets stage a funny swoon.
The monstera giggles and grins,
As it watches everyone with spins.

Lettuce dreams of being gourmet,
While parsley plans to spice the day.
The thyme just laughs; it's not a race,
In this indoor greenery place!

Sanctuary of Shady Corners

Behind the sofa, ferns have grown,
Claiming territory, like it's their throne.
An ivy whispers cheeky lines,
While the rubber plant simply shines.

Cacti wear their prickly smiles,
Competing with the next green miles.
A philodendron leans for fun,
As if this jungle's just begun!

Bamboo stretches, reaching high,
While the pothos waves goodbye.
They know that in this cozy nook,
They'll write the funniest plant book!

The Living Room Jungle

It started small, with just a sprout,
Now it's a jungle; that's no doubt!
A pineapple dreams of sunny shores,
While hibiscus opens its doors.

The couch was once so void and bare,
Now overrun with leafy flair.
A snake plant slithers, causing fright,
While the pothos claims the light!

Laughter rings in leafy halls,
As flowers dance through fragrant calls.
The living room's wild, full of cheer,
Let's greet the plants and bring some beer!

Stems that Dance in Sunshine

In pots where laughter grows,
Stems sway in a floral show.
Curly leaves do a jig,
While roots tease the dancing twig.

Sunbeams do a wiggly waltz,
Plants giggle, yet no faults.
A vine slips on a leaf,
Spinning tales beyond belief.

Petals whisper puns so sweet,
Telling jokes with every beat.
A cactus cracks a smile,
While mushrooms strike a pose for a while.

With every green and blooming bit,
Nature finds her wacky wit.
In this lively, leafy place,
Every plant has room for grace.

The Hidden Garden of Light

Behind the curtains, magic stirs,
With leafy friends and tiny furs.
A sunbeam tickles a fern's hair,
Legend says, it loves a dare.

Basil bursts into a rhyme,
While spider plants mime in time.
A lettuce leaf plays peek-a-boo,
Concealing jokes of what it knew.

Ferns giggle as they sway,
In their green and leafy play.
A daisy tells a corny pun,
Collecting laughter, just for fun.

When dusk falls, the shadows dance,
Plant pals join the merry prance.
Twinkling pots, a lively sight,
In the hidden garden of light.

Serenity in a Terrarium

In eco-jars where the fairies play,
Mossy carpets hide away.
Lichens laugh, they tickle the glass,
As tiny sprigs of green amass.

Peeking through the leafy maze,
Succulents share their sunny ways.
A pebble sings a gentle tune,
Beneath the watchful eye of the moon.

In this globe of calm delight,
Cactus chats with great insight.
A lizard dozes, dreaming of flies,
While plants giggle under the skies.

With every burble, every sigh,
Plants engage in a secret spy.
Whispers of serenity abound,
In this tiny world, joy is found.

Vibrance Within the Walls

Color bursts from every nook,
In pots and shelves, let's take a look.
Foliage sings a joyful sound,
In this vibrant home, joy is found.

Roots twist like a silly dance,
Leaves flutter, oh what a chance!
A rubber plant's sly little grin,
Hints at mischief lurking within.

Bonsai jokes in the corner stand,
In this whimsical green band.
With every sprout, a quip takes flight,
As laughter blooms, my heart feels light.

Walls adorned with nature's art,
For every soul, a playful part.
In this space of green delight,
Every day feels just so right.

A Jungle in the Corner

In the corner lurks a fern,
Whispering secrets, waiting its turn.
Next to it, a cactus so sly,
Claims all the sun, while the herbs sigh.

A spider plant swings with flair,
Dancing . . . but wait, what's that hair?
Did I just see a leaf take a leap?
This jungle's alive, it's never asleep!

The parlor palm plots world domination,
While the pothos shares juicy information.
"Why don't you take a trip," it insists,
"Head outta the pot, find some bliss!"

Mysterious shadows, what could they be?
Are those buds gossiping over tea?
While I sit here, quite unbothered,
My corner is a jungle, a leafy father!

Mossy Corners of Comfort

There's a mossy patch by my bookshelf,
It whispers tales of forgotten wealth.
Books and plants, a cozy respite,
Moss chuckles, "Let's party tonight!"

The succulents gossip, oh what a scene!
"Can you believe I've turned this green?"
While the fairy lights twinkle and blink,
And the pot of gold wishes for a drink!

Each cushion a throne for posh little leaves,
They sip on sunlight and share their heaves.
"Dare to dance?" asks the leaf of jade,
"Join our mossy masquerade!"

With every stretch and every smile,
The room fills up with a lush green style.
As laughter echoes from wall to wall,
In this mossy comfort, we all stand tall!

The Lush Refuge

In my living room, plants hold court,
Laughter erupts as I say, "Pour!"
Fern tips his hat, all suave and slick,
"Ready for a party? Come and pick!"

The rubber tree rolls his eyes with glee,
"Why do they call it plant parenthood, see?
We're the ones teaching you how to grow,
Just follow our lead, it's quite the show!"

Pillows on the floor, a fanciful spread,
While the herbs debate who'll be fed.
"Basil, you can't monopolize the pot!"
"Oh, I'm a guest! Is that really a lot?"

With every new sprout, the giggles erupt,
In my lush refuge, joy is abrupt.
Surrounded by greens, what a surprise,
I find my peace beneath all these skies!

Sprouts of Serenity

In every corner, the sprouts make cheer,
With leafy declarations that ring so clear.
"Let's host a ball, bring the sunlight!"
The potted plants shout, with all their might.

There's a dance of vines, a twist, a turn,
"Oh, who will take the next fern?"
Settings of comfort in every nook,
Could this be the best plant book?

A peace lily nods—"What's your delight?
I'll bloom if the mood is just right."
But the spider plant aims for the role,
"Let's stretch our arms and free our soul!"

As laughter floats in this verdant glade,
Every leaf whispers secrets, unafraid.
In the sprightly setup, life's a feast,
In the green laughter, I find my peace!

Windows to the Wild

In the corner sits a pot,
With dreams of jungle, funny thoughts.
My cat thinks it's a jungle gym,
Chasing shadows on a whim.

The fern waves as I walk by,
I swear it gives a cheeky sigh.
"Water me now!" it seems to say,
As I spin and walk away.

A lizard too, he's quite the chap,
He's dressing up in a leafy wrap.
He finds his throne atop a vine,
Proclaiming, "This room? It's all mine!"

The snake plant strikes a funny pose,
It's tried on every hat that grows.
"Imitation is flattery," it speaks,
In leafy whispers, the plant critiques.

Verdant Haven

A cactus claims the windowsill,
"Don't touch me, or I'll give you a thrill!"
While succulents play hide and seek,
"Who's next?" they tease, "You're looking weak!"

The ivy climbs with mischief bold,
Telling secrets, tales retold.
"Did you see who walked by today?
Stay close, play cool, or just sway!"

Moss spills out like a fuzzy mop,
"Come pet me!" it begs, "Don't you stop!"
The more I touch, the more it laughs,
We share this space, oh how it quaffs!

In this room, chaos reigns supreme,
As plants and laughter weave a dream.
Nature's quirks on full display,
In my cozy green cabaret.

Growth Behind the Glass

Behind my window stands a sprout,
Whispering tales none knew about.
The beetle boasts it bartered skills,
"By tomorrow, I'll climb these hills!"

The peace lily dances to its tune,
"Chasing sunlight, from morn till noon."
But when the shadows stretch and crawl,
It's nap time for one and all.

The potted plant throws a little shade,
"Growing up? Oh, I'll serenade!"
With every inch, a story grows,
In its green heart, the mischief flows.

A sunbeam tickles, just in sight,
The air is thick with pure delight.
This greenery behind the pane,
Is where the humor grows insane!

Ferns and Fables

Oh dear ferns, with stories spun,
You bend and wave, it's so much fun.
They whisper tales of woods and streams,
While I sip my herbal dreams.

In shadows deep, a gnome appears,
He's juggling leaves, igniting cheers!
"Could I borrow a cup of soil?"
He winks and leaves me with his toil.

There's laughter here, in every vine,
Peeking from pots, they intertwine.
A spider plant spins webs of glee,
"Watch out, a tree might sprout from me!"

So here I sit, with joy amassed,
In leafy worlds, my heart is cast.
Fables told by ferns so green,
Where laughter blooms, a playful scene.

Fern Fronds and Fuzzy Socks

In my living room, plants do dance,
Waving their fronds, they take a chance.
Fuzzy socks keep my toes warm,
As feral ferns spread their charm.

Potted ways with a splash of glee,
They whisper secrets, just to me.
Overgrown jungles in every nook,
Who knew that leaves could write a book?

With soil-stained fingers and giggles galore,
I chat with greens, demanding more.
They lean a bit closer, just to hear,
My tales of mischief, loud and clear.

Oh, fuzzy socks and ferns in sight,
Turn my shadows into light.
While I sip tea and park my toes,
They mime ballet with swaying prose.

Where Nature Meets Nurture

In my corner sits a cactus proud,
I tell it jokes, it laughs out loud.
Succulents love my witty jest,
They peek from pots, all dressed in zest.

Pothos trails down like a green parade,
Got no idea it's just stayed stayed!
With quirky leaves that twist and curl,
It's definitely the best of my world.

The potted pals all gather 'round,
Plant debates—they're quite renowned.
Why care for soil? Why not just dance?
They'll sway in sunlight, given a chance!

While I drink coffee, conjuring schemes,
They concoct plans with funny dreams.
In this room where foliage thrives,
Who knew household buddies could be wise?

Green Shadows of Solitude

In my lap, a spider plant sprawls,
While a chubby snail makes its calls.
Cacti laugh at my snail's slow pace,
As shadows stretch, they join the race.

My cozy nook is now a hub,
For leafy gossip, jokes, and snub.
Where big-leafed giants plot and scheme,
Mossy cushions join the dream.

Please don't disturb my tree's sad face,
It frowns at all the empty space.
But when the light is just right,
Their leafy smiles emerge with delight.

The stillness hums a quirky tune,
As sunshine dances, bright as noon.
With shadowy friends, I'm not alone,
In my green bubble, I've truly grown.

Leafy Comforts in Cozy Spaces

My room's a jungle of leafy hearts,
Where poor spiders are true master arts.
A fern in flippers takes a dive,
While I snicker, feeling alive.

The peace lilies gossip with no end,
Over tea and cookies, they're quite a blend.
Fuzzy creatures underfoot roam,
Beneath a canopy, they build a home.

Bamboo shoots believe they can sing,
Twirling in rhythm, oh what a fling!
My cushions laugh, they can't sit still,
In this chaotic green-filled thrill.

So here I sit, a smirk on my face,
With leafy companions, I've found my place.
In the dance of plants and cozy grins,
I find myself, true joy begins.

Threading Green in Tranquility

In pots they chat and giggle, too,
My leafy friends, a vibrant crew.
They wave their leaves, a silly dance,
Who knew plants could have such a chance?

They argue about the sunniest spot,
While I wonder if they've got a plot.
I fear one day they'll plot a coup,
And turn my home into a zoo!

In soil they burrow, roots below,
While Photosynthesis steals the show.
With chlorophyll and a wink of glee,
My apartment feels like a comedy spree!

So here's to greens, with laughter thrown,
In tranquil spaces, we've all grown!
Between the ferns, who needs a screen?
My home's transformed, a leafy scene!

Captured in Greenery

The cactus sways, a spiky tease,
While orchids laugh with fragrant ease.
A fern throws shade, a chilling vibe,
As potted dreams begin to vibe.

The philodendron wears a grin,
While succulents are plotting sin.
Who will spill the dirt today?
Just hope they don't grow legs and stray!

A rescue mission for a wilted leaf,
The drama builds, oh what a grief!
With watering cans, we wage a fight,
Against neglect, we'll save the night!

In this indoor jungle, laughter thrives,
Where every plant, it truly strives.
So come and join this leafy spree,
In this greenery, we're all carefree!

The Blooming Heart of the Home

In the corner sits my blooming mate,
With flowers bright and jokes first rate.
I swear I heard it chuckle loud,
Giving blooms like a vibrant crowd!

The tongue plant claims the brightest chair,
While geraniums spread gossip rare.
They whisper secrets of their plight,
While I provide the late-night light.

A sunflower sneezes—oh dear me!
It startled the cat up in the tree.
With every petal, laughter spills,
In this house, it's joy that thrills!

So let us raise a glass to greens,
In every pot, the laughter beams.
From flower to leaf, let's share the tone,
In my heart, they're never alone!

Indoor Wilderness Enchantment

I've made a forest right indoors,
With tiny trees and happy doors.
The orchids wave, a merry band,
While violets are making a stand!

A mischievous vine stretches wide,
Pulling curtains with leafy pride.
The cat climbs high, thinks she's a queen,
In this wild, leafy scene, it's seen!

A hanging pot of giggles blooms,
As sunlight spills in, light consumes.
They chat and joke in verdant style,
While I just shake my head and smile.

So here's to my wild patch of cheer,
Where plants and laughter gather near.
In this enchanted indoor ground,
Every corner bursts with joy unbound!

Nature's Palette at Home

My cactus wears a sun hat tight,
It claims it's ready for a day of light.
The fern in the corner sways with glee,
Saying, "Why not join my leafy spree?"

The pot of basil thinks it's quite grand,
Waving its leaves like a rock band.
"Basil's the spice that thrills the taste,
While I just sit here, what a waste!"

The succulent jokes about being tough,
Saying, "Life is easier when you're not rough!"
While the ivy is climbing higher to tease,
"Catch me if you can, with all your ease!"

As I laugh with my plants, my heart takes flight,
Nature's palette within my sight.
In this little jungle, joy does bloom,
Who knew my home was a plant-filled room?

Comfort in Chlorophyll

Under the glow of my lamp so bright,
Plants share secrets in the pale moonlight.
The pothos chuckles, his vines entwined,
"I'm just here to keep you in good mind!"

The spider plant is bold, spreading its cheer,
"Why worry, my friend? Just open your beer!"
While the peace lily sighs, a potent spell,
"I'm your guardian; all will be well!"

With soil on my hands, I fear not the mess,
Each plant reminds me that life's a success.
Their green whispers dance through the air,
In every corner, they spread love and care.

At night, they plot their great escape,
Through windows and doors, they would reshape.
Yet here they stay, my leafy crew,
In our little world, we flourish anew!

Leafy Friends by the Fireside

By the warm fire, my friends do gather,
Each leaf speaks, causing hearty laughter.
The rubber plant shows off its flair,
"I'm the superstar; just look at my hair!"

The dracaena pipes up with a wink,
"Motivational speeches? Let me speak, think!"
While the ferns in their dresses sway free,
"We're the fashionistas of this plant party!"

A little watering can joins the fun,
"Don't drown us now; we're not ready to run!"
Laughter erupts; the leaves get tickled,
"My soil's too dry; I'm feeling a little beamed!"

So here we bask in our chlorophyll cheer,
With all of my plants, it's quite clear.
Life's an amusing, leafy delight,
Together in warmth, our hearts take flight!

The Soil Beneath the Floor

Beneath the floor, a mystery brews,
Little roots whispering secret news.
"What's happening above? Are they having fun?"
"I hope they're not out in the sun!"

A lone worm twirls in the rich dark clay,
"I'm the party planner for this earthy stay!"
While the potting mix laughs, feeling so grand,
"I'm the VIP; let me make my stand!"

The mysterious fungi are hosting a drum,
"Just listen to us; we'll make your heart hum!"
While the little stones chuckle in their place,
"We're here to keep the pace in grace!"

Imagine their tales as they dream and plot,
Our little garden party, it means a lot.
For life underground is a jolly affair,
Full of laughter and whispers, with love to share!

Echoes of Nature's Chorus

In my living room, a plant takes a seat,
Wearing a hat made of wool and some feet.
Telling the cat to stop giving it stares,
While sipping on sunlight and sharing some cares.

A fern jiggles nervously, dances with glee,
As I hum along to its photosynthesis spree.
The couch joins in, creaking with style,
While cushions are grooving, oh, what a while!

The cactus is quiet, a spiky old chap,
Whispers of wisdom from his prickly wrap.
A gathering of leaves, a botanical bash,
As we all reminisce about last night's trash!

So come one, come all, let the green party spread,
With petals and laughter, let's dance 'til we're red.
In this quirky jungle where joy fills the air,
Nature's little chorus sings—if you're aware!

Embracing Earthly Vibes

My potted pals are quite the scene,
Chatting in whispers, calm and serene.
The ivy creeps up like a curious spy,
Peeking at me with its leafy sly eye.

Each morning I wake to the sounds of their cheer,
The basil is buzzing, "Just bring me some beer!"
The ferns gossip softly, their voices so light,
About how to stretch out and dance through the night.

A garden of chatter, a riot of green,
Where laughter erupts like a fresh, playful sheen.
The rubber plant boasts of its shiny new leaf,
While saying, "Oh please, spare me your grief!"

Socks tangled about with a pot inspired flair,
As dirt stains the carpet, I simply don't care.
With Earth in my grasp and a smile on my face,
This funny green twist has become my own space!

Sprouting Hopes Inside

In a small corner, the seedlings awake,
Dreaming of sunshine and how to partake.
"Who needs the outdoors?" they squeak with delight,
"As long as the fridge is stocked up tight!"

The spider plant sidles, so sly and so spry,
Winking at me with that innocent eye.
"Let's throw a party, where's the disco ball?"
As we shimmy and shake, not a one feels too small!

Lettuce and laughter blend into green smoothies,
Dressing up veggies in fashionable booties.
The herbs form a band, with a rhythm divine,
Jamming to music that's organic, just fine!

Oh, tiny joys flourish in pots all around,
With each little sprout, hidden giggles abound.
A feast of faux fun in this lively domain,
Sprouting new hopes in their slapstick campaign!

Lushness Behind Doors

Behind closed doors, a jungle exists,
With pots of green joy and sunshine's twist.
The aloe plants gossip, it's quite a charade,
Sharing their secrets, like old masquerade.

The peace lily's jokes make the bright sunlight laugh,
While succulents gather for a selfie half-staff.
"Say cheese!" they shout with a leafy surprise,
As shadows dance joyfully beneath close skies.

Vines wrap around chairs, making them snug,
While critters in clay pots poke in for a hug.
The laughter resounds through the terracotta walls,
As nature gets silly and spontaneity calls!

So here in my haven, where green antics soar,
I celebrate flora, and what's even more,
I'm joined by these friends in a giggly brigade,
Embracing the lushness that never will fade!

Raindrops on the Window Pane

Raindrops dance and play,
Like tiny drummers on parade.
Each one's a silly clown,
Creating smiles all around.

The cat jumps up and swipes,
At streams of water running wild.
He thinks he's on a quest,
A brave and daring child.

Puddles form and quack,
The ducks all wish to splash.
They waddle in their raincoats,
Creating quite a bash!

With every drop that falls,
The world gets fresh and bright.
This silly watery show,
Brings pure delight, what a sight!

Silent Symphony of Fronds

Fronds are waving gently,
In a quiet, leafy dance.
They sway and tease the air,
As if they're in romance.

A spider spins a web,
With threads of silver sheen.
It's a sticky instrument,
In this leafy, funny scene.

The fern gives a little giggle,
As it brushes past the wall.
A chorus of green whispers,
That really make me smile.

In this jungle of my home,
Nature's laughter fills the air.
With leafy friends around me,
Who wouldn't stop and stare?

Whispers of Nature's Touch

In every corner hiding,
A plant that thinks it's bold.
With leaves that peek and giggle,
Green stories waiting to be told.

Cacti wear their spines,
Like crowns upon their heads.
Roses gossip to the daisies,
From their cozy flower beds.

The herbs are planning mischief,
In their little pot town.
They season up the laughter,
With joy instead of frowns.

Like tiny green comedians,
In this little indoor space.
Each leaf a little joker,
Ready for a humored chase!

The Green Thumb's Secret

With muddy hands I dig,
Planting seeds with great delight.
My plants are like my children,
They giggle through the night.

The neighbor thinks I'm crazy,
For talking to my thyme.
But every sprout is listening,
As I whisper every rhyme.

My watering can sings loudly,
It chats with every bloom.
While earthworms wriggle softly,
In their little underground room.

To cultivate more laughter,
Is truly my intent.
In this quirky green domain,
The joy is evident!